EDGE
BOOKS™

Not Your Ordinary Trivia

HOLLYWOOD TRIVIA

What You never Knew About Celebrity Life, Fame, and Fortune

by Elizabeth Weitzman

CAPSTONE PRESS
a capstone imprint

Edge Books are published by Capstone Press,
1710 Roe Crest Drive, North Mankato, Minnesota 56003
www.mycapstone.com

Library of Congress Cataloging-in-Publication Data
Names: Weitzman, Elizabeth, author.
Title: Hollywood trivia : what you never knew about celebrity life, fame,
and fortune / by Elizabeth Weitzman.
Description: Mankato, Minnesota : Edge Books, [2019] | Series: Edge books.
  not your ordinary trivia. | Includes bibliographical references and
index.
Identifiers: LCCN 2018005780 (print) | LCCN 2018008516 (ebook) | ISBN
  9781543525366 (eBook PDF) | ISBN 9781543525403 (ePub Fixed Layout) |
  ISBN 9781543525281 (library binding : alk. paper) | ISBN 9781543525328
  (pbk. : alk. paper)
Subjects: LCSH: Motion picture industry—California—Los
  Angeles—Miscellanea. | Motion picture actors and
  actresses—California—Los Angeles—Miscellanea. | Motion picture
  producers and directors—California—Los Angeles—Miscellanea.
Classification: LCC PN1998 (ebook) | LCC PN1998 .W35 2019 (print) | DDC
  791.4309794/94—dc23
LC record available at https://lccn.loc.gov/2018005780

Editorial Credits
Amanda Robbins, editor; Juliette Peters, designer; Jo Miller, media researcher;
Tori Abraham, production specialist

Photo Credits
Alamy: AF archive, 10l, AF archive, 20, Ian G Dagnall, 9; Getty Images: Archive Photos/Stringer,
22t, Fred Duval/Contributor, 18, Julian Wasser/Contributor, 22b, Kevin Winter/Staff, 21t, Keystone-
France/Contributoir, 14, Venturelli/Contributor, 28t; Newscom: CelebrityHomePhotos/Carrillo, 12t,
Courtesy of ABC Family/ZUMA Press, 29; David Longendyke, 24t, Emilio Flores, 25, NEW LINE
PRODUCTIONS/Album, 17t, Reuters/Gary Hershorn, 23; Shutterstock: Africa Studio, 6, Aperture75,
11b, BrunoGarridoMacias, 16, Crystal Eye Studio, 28b, DenisNata, 19tl, djgis, 15b, eakkachai halang, 17b,
FeatureFlash Photo Agency, 13tl, 19b, 27t, Francey, 10r, gresei, 27b, Halay Alex, 24b, hugolacasse, cover, IM_
photo, 7, Ingus Kruklitis, 8t, Irina Maksimova, 19tr, Jeremy Fougerouse, 8b, Kathy Hutchins, 26l, Matthew
Connolly, 13b, Netfalls Remy Musser, 15t, Pongpachara Ratsameechand, 13tr, Rich Carey, 19tm, rkjaer, 21b,
Sean Pavone, 4-5, SkillUp, 11b, SPF, 11t, Twocoms, 26r, Wire_man, 12b

Design Elements
Shutterstock: hugolacasse

Printed in the United States of America.
PA017

Table of Contents

Welcome to Hollywood!

Hollywood is where actors and **directors** create fairy tales and fantasies on screen. It's also a place where they live them!

People who make movies work long hours, and some earn huge paychecks. Some of their cars cost more than half a million dollars. That's more than most people's houses. Celebrity houses might be as big as your school! Some stars even own private planes.

Hollywood is a glamorous town. Millions of people visit Hollywood each year to tour the city for themselves. But there's more to Hollywood than meets the eye. Are you ready for a behind-the-scenes tour? Get the inside scoop about a real-life wonderland filled with movie stars, mansions, and million-dollar parties.

director—the person who is in charge of a movie

CHAPTER 1

Hollywood History

"Hollywood" refers to an area in Los Angeles, California, where movies are made. But it can also describe the film itself. The business of moviemaking has been around for about 125 years. It's gone through a lot of changes in that time.

In the early 1900s, the first movies looked very different from the ones made today. They were made in black and white instead of color. Each film was only a few minutes long. They didn't even have sound! They were called silent films.

Early movies weren't made in Hollywood. Most were made in France, New York City, and New Jersey. But it's tough to make movies year-round in places that have snowy winters. Filmmakers soon started moving out to sunny Los Angeles. Producers made the first Hollywood movie in 1910. Before long, many others followed.

Los Angeles is Spanish for "The Angels." That's easier to say than the town's original name. It was *El Pueblo de Nuestra Señora la Reina de los Ángeles del Río Porciúncula.* That means "Town of Our Lady the Queen of Angels of the River Porciúncula." The name was shortened by the early 1800s.

You may already know that Thomas Edison helped mass produce the light bulb. Did you know he had a part in inventing America's first movie camera too? Edison and William Dickson invented what they called the Kinetograph. Edison also built the country's first movie **studio** near his home in New Jersey.

studio—a place where movies, television shows, and radio shows are made

How will you know when you arrive in Hollywood? There's a giant sign to tell you. Each letter is about 45 feet (14 meters) high and 33 feet (10 m) wide. The whole sign weighs about 480,000 pounds (217,724 kilograms). That's as heavy as 20 school buses!

HOLLYWOODLAND

When the Hollywood sign was put up in 1923, it said "Hollywoodland." About 20 years later, it was in terrible shape. By then, people around the world knew the town as "Hollywood." A new sign was made to replace it in 1949, but the last four letters were left off.

In 1953 a group of Hollywood businessmen wanted to honor the celebrities who were making their town famous. Five years later, they began adding stars to the sidewalk on Hollywood Boulevard. Each star represented a beloved entertainer. Today more than 2,600 stars cover 15 sidewalks. This stretch is called the Hollywood Walk of Fame. You'll find everyone from Walt Disney to Johnny Depp represented there. There are even stars for Snoopy, Shrek, and Godzilla!

It's a big deal to be invited to have a star on the Walk of Fame. But celebrities have to pay for them. And at $30,000 each, they don't come cheap!

CHAPTER 2

Show Me the Money

When the first movie theater opened in 1905, a ticket cost only a nickel. Today tickets cost about $9. That's almost 200 times more! And that's not the only dollar amount that's gotten bigger over the years.

In 1938 Judy Garland made $500 a week to play Dorothy in *The Wizard of Oz*. The dog who played her pet, Toto, earned $125 a week!

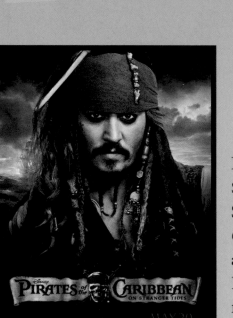

In 2011 Johnny Depp was paid $55 million to play Captain Jack Sparrow in *Pirates of the Caribbean: On Stranger Tides*. The movie broke a record for the most expensive Hollywood film ever. It cost $410.6 million to make. But it earned more than $1 billion!

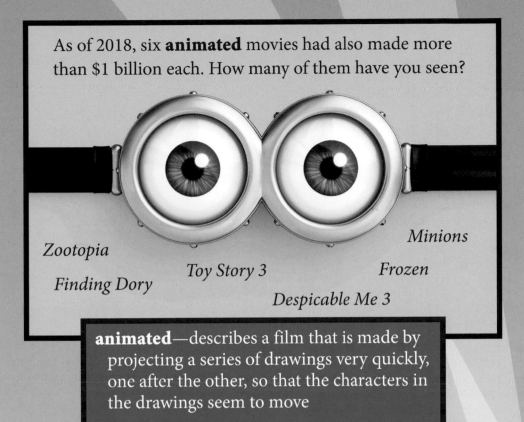

As of 2018, six **animated** movies had also made more than $1 billion each. How many of them have you seen?

Zootopia

Finding Dory

Toy Story 3

Despicable Me 3

Minions

Frozen

animated—describes a film that is made by projecting a series of drawings very quickly, one after the other, so that the characters in the drawings seem to move

In 1977 director George Lucas was sure his original *Star Wars* movie was going to flop. Embarrassed, Lucas went on vacation to Hawaii when the movie was released. No one was more surprised than he was when *Star Wars* earned more than $300 million in theaters. At the time, that was more than any other movie had ever made.

Hollywood is packed with expensive, over-the-top mansions. Reality TV star Kim Kardashian and hip-hop artist Kanye West shared an $11 million house. It had a bowling alley, a movie theater, and a basketball court. There was a giant garage for Kim's $325,000 Ferrari and Kanye's $440,000 Lamborghini. They even had $750,000 gold-plated toilets. The couple sold the home in 2017 for $17.8 million.

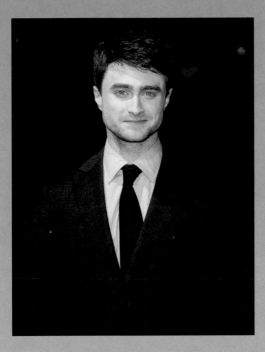

Daniel Radcliffe made more than $70 million for playing Harry Potter in all eight movies. He's tried to save most of his money. But he did once spend $17,000 on a mattress.

Hogwarts

Unlike Radcliffe, famed actor Nicolas Cage is a pretty big spender. His film credits go back almost 40 years. While some celebrities buy mansions, Cage owned two castles. He also had two islands, a pet octopus, and a comic book worth $150,000! At one point Cage almost had to file bankruptcy.

CHAPTER 3

MOVIE MAGIC

Hundreds of people work on a movie before it gets to theaters. Check out some of the secrets you won't see onscreen.

Every movie is put together **scene** by scene. In 1931 actor and director Charlie Chaplin made his popular comedy *City Lights*. He reshot one scene 342 times.

scene—a part of a story, play, or movie that shows what is happening in one place and time

Many movies are set in one city, but shot in another. The 2016 movie *Ghostbusters* is set in New York. That movie was actually filmed in Boston, Massachusetts. *Spider-Man: Homecoming* is supposed to take place in New York City. It was actually shot in Atlanta, Georgia, and Los Angeles, California, instead. Iceland often stands in for outer space. Parts of *Star Trek: Into Darkness*, *Star Wars: The Force Awakens*, and *Rogue One: A Star Wars Story* were all shot there.

Next time you watch an action movie, pay close attention to the lead actor or actress. If you can't see his or her face, it might be because someone else is playing the part. Stunt people take over when a scene is dangerous. They're trained to race cars or jump off buildings. They don't get the fame, but they do get to do the coolest stuff!

Some actors do their own stunts, but it can be risky! Jackie Chan does all of his dangerous fight scenes. He's broken his skull, most of his fingers, his ankle, and his cheekbone. He's also broken his nose four times.

Movies have shown space fights, dragons, and hurricanes. How do filmmakers create such scenes? They use **computer generated imagery (CGI)**. These special effects are added by computers after a movie is made. Take Iron Man's awesome armor. During shooting, actor Robert Downey Jr. was usually just wearing a tight red bodysuit. Then it was transformed into armor by CGI.

computer generated imagery (CGI)—a way to make special effects using a computer

Actor Andy Serkis specializes in CGI-based characters. For these roles he does all his acting in a special suit. It covers his body with sensors that record his movements. Once a scene is filmed, CGI animation can transform the way he looks. That's how he was able to play the creepy creature Gollum in the *Lord of the Rings* and *Hobbit* movies. It's also how he became the title monster in *King Kong* and the ape leader of the *Planet of the Apes* films. He also played Supreme Leader Snoke in the *Star Wars* movies.

Most films with special effects also use green screens. These look like plain green backgrounds while a movie is being made. When you watch characters running away from spaceships or villains, they're probably inside a studio. Or they might be on an empty city street. And they're running from . . . nothing! Backgrounds are added later.

In movies, things aren't always what they appear to be. When you see Hogwarts school in a Harry Potter movie, you're often looking at a model that's about 50 feet (15.2 m) wide. The whole thing fits inside a single room! The beds that Harry and his best friend Ron use are tiny. By the end of the series, the actors' legs hung off the ends of the beds. The filmmakers left that part off screen.

Special effects also include sounds. In *Jurassic Park* the sounds of angry dinosaurs are horses, geese, and baby elephants.

DRAX

MARVEL
RDIANS

Makeup goes a long way toward creating a fantasy. It took makeup artists five hours every morning to turn Dave Bautista into the alien warrior Drax for *Guardians of the Galaxy*. It took another hour and a half to take off all his makeup at the end of each day.

super celebrations

Hollywood is party central! Every week there are celebrations, from **premieres** to wrap bashes and awards shows. These events are great excuses for actors to put on expensive suits and designer dresses!

premiere—the first public performance of a film, play, or work of music or dance

Movies take months to make and involve hundreds of people. When filming is done, the cast and **crew** have a big party. They may give each other "wrap gifts." After Adam Sandler made the comedy *Grown Ups*, he gave his castmates new cars!

crew—a team of people who work together behind the scenes to produce a movie

Once a movie is ready for the public to see, filmmakers throw a premiere party. Big premiere parties can cost millions of dollars. One of the most expensive premieres in history was for *Pearl Harbor*. Two thousand people attended the $5 million party. It was held on a naval ship in Hawaii. The event included nearly $1 million worth of fireworks!

The most important night in Hollywood is the Academy Awards. The event is also called the Oscars. This program awards people who made the best movies of the year. The first Oscars were held in 1929. That ceremony lasted 15 minutes and was attended by 270 people. Now it costs about $40 million to plan the event. Around 3,400 people pack the theater. More than 30 million others watch the show on TV.

Many people have won more than one Oscar. But so far Walt Disney had the most. By the end of his career, he'd won 22 trophies.

Tatum O'Neal was the youngest actor to win an Oscar. She was just 10 when she earned the Academy Award for Best Supporting Actress. She played Addie Loggins in the 1973 movie *Paper Moon.* Her real dad, Ryan O'Neal, played her father in the movie.

The Academy Awards are Hollywood's fanciest night of the year. But the funniest is probably the Golden Raspberry Awards. At this ceremony trophies called Razzies are given to actors of the year's worst movies. Sandra Bullock once won an Oscar and a Razzie in the same weekend for two different films. The Razzie was for a comedy called *All About Steve*. The Oscar was for a drama called *The Blind Side*.

The money that goes
into an actor's wardrobe
at the Academy Awards
can be mind-blowing.
Nicole Kidman once
wore a necklace worth
$7 million to the Oscars.
It had 7,500 diamonds
in it and took more than
6,000 hours to make!

At the 2013 Oscars, Jennifer
Lawrence wore a gown worth
$4 million. Unfortunately, the
dress was too long. When she
went on stage to accept her
award, she tripped!

A **nomination** for an Academy Award is a big honor. It also comes with gift bags. Past gifts have included diamond jewelry, bicycles, and surfing lessons. Other gifts were trips to Hawaii, Italy, and Japan.

nominate—to name someone as a candidate for an award

After the Oscars are over, the guests go to the biggest party of the year. It's called the Governor's Ball. Hundreds of chefs work for weeks to prepare the food. Past menus have included soup with real gold flakes and corn dogs stuffed with lobster. A dessert buffet table spans the entire room. It's filled with sweets from caramel lollipops to 7,000 mini chocolate Oscar statues.

star surprises

You see Hollywood's biggest stars in your favorite movies and TV shows. Sometimes it may feel like you know them. But there's still a lot more to learn. Remember these fun facts the next time you see these celebrities on-screen.

Hugh Jackman

Gal Gadot

Actors usually have other jobs before they get into the movie business. Hugh Jackman became very famous after his star role as Wolverine in the *X-Men* movies. But he worked as a gym teacher and a party clown before that. Israeli actress Gal Gadot was a soldier in her country's army before she starred as Wonder Woman.

Actors move to Hollywood because that's where they work. But many grew up far from L.A. Hugh Jackman, Nicole Kidman, and Naomi Watts are Australian. Charlize Theron is from South Africa. Ryan Gosling, Rachel McAdams, and Jim Carrey are Canadian. Amy Adams was born in Italy. Emma Watson was born in Paris, France.

Some actors seem like they'd be all wrong for their roles. Johnny Depp played candymaker Willy Wonka in *Charlie and the Chocolate Factory*. In real life, he was allergic to chocolate when he was a kid. Luckily, he outgrew his allergy. James Earl Jones is celebrated now as the voice of *Star Wars* villain Darth Vader. But he stuttered so badly as a child that he barely spoke.

Stars don't just spend their money on fast cars and huge houses. Many of them work hard to make the world a better place. Oscar-winning actor Leonardo DiCaprio has his own charity. He is especially dedicated to helping animals and the environment. The Leonardo DiCaprio Foundation works to protect oceans, forests, and other places from climate change.

Harrison Ford is most famous for playing *Star Wars* pilot Han Solo. But he's a pilot in real life too. Ford owns several planes, which he uses to help people in need. He even flew supplies to Haiti after the country had a terrible earthquake in 2010.

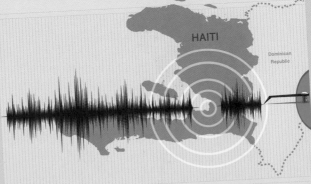

Some stars get tired of the Hollywood life. They happily give up fame to do something else. Peter Ostrum played Charlie in the 1971 version of *Willy Wonka & the Chocolate Factory*. Then he decided acting wasn't for him. He grew up to become a veterinarian instead.

Does Hollywood sound like somewhere you'd like to live? It's a crazy place with weird, wild, and wonderful surprises around every corner. And now that you know some of the secrets behind the scenes, you may never look at movies the same way again!

Glossary

animated (AN-i-may-tid)—describes a film that is made by projecting a series of drawings very quickly, one after the other, so that the characters in the drawings seem to move

computer generated imagery (kuhm-PYOO-tur JEN-uh-ray-tud IM-ij-ree)—a way to make special effects using a computer; also called CGI

crew (CROO)—a team of people who work together behind the scenes to produce a movie or TV show

director (duh-REK-tuhr)—the person who is in charge of a movie

industry (IN-duh-stree)—a single branch of business or trade

nominate (NOM-uh-nate)—to name someone as a candidate for an award

premiere (pruh-MIHR)—the first public performance of a film, play, or work of music or dance

producer (pruh-DOO-ser)—a person who puts the many parts of a movie together.

scene (SEEN)—a part of a story, play, or movie that shows what is happening in one place and time

studio (STOO-dee-oh)—a place where movies, television shows, and radio shows are made

wrap (RAP)—the completed filming of a scene in a movie or TV show

Read More

Fields, Jan. *Asking Questions About How Hollywood Movies Get Made.* Asking Questions About Media. Ann Arbor, Mich.: Cherry Lake Publishing, 2016.

Hammelef, Danielle. *Eye-Popping CGI: Computer-Generated Special Effects.* Awesome Special Effects. North Mankato, Minn.: Capstone Press, 2015.

Stoller, Bryan Michael. *Smartphone Movie Maker.* Somerville, Mass.: Candlewick Press, 2017.

Internet Sites

Use FactHound to find Internet sites related to this book.

Visit *www.facthound.com*

Just type in 9781543525281 and go.

Index